10 STEPS TO OWNING YOUR OWN TRUCKING FREIGHT BROKER/AGENT BUSINESS

Alicia Griffin

CW Ransom

Bethel Business Solutions Transforming Dreams Into Reality

10 STEPS TO OWNING YOUR OWN TRUCKING FREIGHT BROKER/ AGENT BUSINESS

10 STEPS TO A CAREER IN THE
TRANSPORTATION BROKERAGE INDUSTRY
Copyright @ 2014 by Alicia Productions, Inc.

ALL RIGHTS RESERVED. This book contains material protected under International and Federal Copyright Laws and Treaties. Any unauthorized reprint or use of this material is prohibited. No part of this book may be reproduced or transmitted in any form or by any means, electronic o mechanical, including
photocopying, recording, or by any information storage and retrieval system without expressed written permission or the author/publisher.

Cover Design: D Media District
Freight Broker: Tamara Roberts
Revised : October 2015

ISBN: 978-0-9893295-3-8
Printed in the USA

Copyright @ Alicia Productions Inc. 2014

Bethel Business Solutions Transforming Dreams Into Reality

10 STEPS TO OWNING YOUR OWN TRUCKING FREIGHT BROKER/ AGENT BUSINESS

Table of Contents

Greetings

Step 1 Define the role of the Broker and Agent

Step 2 Learn how the Industry Works

Step 3 Abide by the Industry's Standards

Step 4 Satisfy the steps to Become an Agent

Step 5 Understand the Industry's Work Environment

Step 6 Familiarize Yourself with Industry Terms

Step 7 Build the Steps to Become a Broker

Step 8 Consider the Big Picture

Step 9 Discover Self-Pace &Time Management Success

Step 10 Solutions - Bethel Business Solutions

Bethel Business Solutions Transforming Dreams Into Reality

10 STEPS TO OWNING YOUR OWN TRUCKING FREIGHT BROKER/ AGENT BUSINESS

Greetings!

Welcome to the one of the nation's largest growing careers in the transportation industry. The transportation industry presently accounts for over five million persons employed in logistics. Positions include truck drivers, mechanics – and one of the most profitable career choices is as a transportation broker/agent.

We have designed this booklet to provide you with some basic knowledge for your new career choice, exciting job descriptions of the broker and agent, and a general overview of the transportation industry.

Bethel Business Solutions Transforming Dreams Into Reality

10 STEPS TO OWNING YOUR OWN TRUCKING FREIGHT BROKER/ AGENT BUSINESS

Our goal is to provide you the opportunity to move forward with logistic training where you will gain more information for a career move that offers unlimited earning potential. **Ask me how?** Visit my website at: www.bethelbusinesssolutions.com. Wishing you great success,

Alicia Griffin
Author

Bethel Business Solutions Transforming Dreams Into Reality

10 STEPS TO OWNING YOUR OWN TRUCKING FREIGHT BROKER/ AGENT BUSINESS

STEP ONE
Define the role of the Broker and Agent

Are you stuck in a dead end job and looking for a way out? Perhaps you have no job at all? Maybe owning your own company is what you are most passionate about.

Well, you've have come to the right place. While the freight and transportation business may not be for everyone, there's the possibility that this is the **gold mine** and **goal mind** you've been searching for.

Entrepreneur Magazine has rated the freight brokerage business as one of the top home-based businesses to own. A recent Wall Street Journal article cited freight brokering and logistics as the largest growing sector of the transportation industry. Let me tell you more about the ever growing industry of freight brokerage company and process agent career.

The transportation brokerage industry has experienced exponential growth over the past thirty years. **Many shippers face the challenge of seeking opportunities to establish relationships with reliable freighters. It is the goal of both the shipper and carrier to work hard to get freight moved. Being able to solve the problem and get reliable and consistent transportation in the marketplace is the goal of all in the freight and transportation business.**

Challenging issues freighters are facing include limitations of seasonal issues and

Bethel Business Solutions Transforming Dreams Into Reality

10 STEPS TO OWNING YOUR OWN TRUCKING FREIGHT BROKER/ AGENT BUSINESS

specialized freight handling requirements. As a result, a number of challenges exist for both the carrier and shippers.

Advantages of Working Under a Brokerage Agency

Are there advantages to a position as a transportation broker or agent in the transportation industry? How about owning a brokerage company? **Brokers are specialists who have expertise at moving freight in an efficient and professional manner with rates negotiated on a load-by-load basis with the carrier.**

The answer is yes, most definitely.

While starting you won agency is financially beneficial, there are many benefits of working for a brokerage agency.

- The work that goes into a business start-up can be tremendous and labor intensive.

- The trust confident business relationship between carriers, shippers and other brokerage firms in the logistic industry are close to impossible to establish for the new company that is just starting up.

- Other advantages include low overhead and start-up cost of operating a freight brokerage agency. Here are a few of the benefits working under a brokerage agency bring to the table.

Bethel Business Solutions Transforming Dreams Into Reality

10 STEPS TO OWNING YOUR OWN TRUCKING FREIGHT BROKER/ AGENT BUSINESS

- The cost of liability insurance may not be a hindrance but the chances of a new company being able to secure a general liability policy may prove difficult – almost impossible.

- It is important to have additional insurance coverage just in case a loss or damage occurs that the carrier's insurance does not cover. While the law does not require a company to hold a Contingent Cargo policy, it is highly recommended and expenses.

- Other costs and added expenses associated with the freight brokerage company that are not absorbed by an agent includes surety bond. The surety bond may not be expensive, but it is an additional expense.

- Another additional expense includes a marketing plan.

- The checks and balances necessary in the transportation freight company are a gateway to a successful business.

- The experience gained by working with an existing freight company can provide the internal workings necessary for a successful brokerage company. Take advantage of this eye opening experience and situate yourself in a position to "learn while you earn."

Bethel Business Solutions Transforming Dreams Into Reality

10 STEPS TO OWNING YOUR OWN TRUCKING FREIGHT BROKER/ AGENT BUSINESS

- A potential agent working under the leadership and training of a brokerage firm will not be responsible for any of the cost associated with the agency. It is the job of the agent to secure freight and cover the shipper's transportation needs.

- The firm supplies resources for all expenses with no charges to the agent.

- Most brokerage firms will offer an agent a lucrative percentage of the net profits or a smaller percentage of the growth revenue.

- In a typical situation, the agent is able to ask for increased commission as the level of knowledge and experience increases.

Starting a brokerage allows you to profit by matching carriers with available capacity to shippers needs in the transportation services.

Owning your own business can be exciting and rewarding with untold advantages. We have all dreamed of being our own boss, setting our own schedule and doing something that we love calling it work.

Well, working as a Transportation Broker or Agent is working as your own boss! You will be able to set your own schedule, work from a home-based office as long as you have your own computer, computer system, company software, fax, and telephone.

Bethel Business Solutions Transforming Dreams Into Reality

10 STEPS TO OWNING YOUR OWN TRUCKING FREIGHT BROKER/ AGENT BUSINESS

Some of the necessary key qualities that have proven beneficial in owning your own business include dedication, hard work, successful planning, implementing of the plan, review, and revision of the plan. Other ingredients for a successful business include finances, resources, and man or woman power. So now, let's get started.

Bethel Business Solutions Transforming Dreams Into Reality

10 STEPS TO OWNING YOUR OWN TRUCKING FREIGHT BROKER/ AGENT BUSINESS

STEP TWO
Here's How the Industry Works

Everything must move. From the manufacturer to the marketplace somehow and the general movement of freight and cargo by motor carriage will be our focus. The general movement of truckload freight from origin to destination can be broken into three main components.

The first component of the process is created by a shipper, a manufacturer, a distributor, or a wholesaler. The shipper must acquire freight transportation services so its products or items can be delivered to its customers.

The second component of the transaction includes a broker or brokerage company who helps to arrange for the transportation services to be executed.

Component three of the process is the carrier, who has transportation capabilities and a vehicle with which to complete the movement of the freight from origin to destination. Sometimes shippers contact the carrier directly, they agree to a rate, sign a carriage contract and deal with each other directly.

However, any shippers may wish to focus solely on the business at hand and outsource or use an intermediary or broker to assist with the logistics needs.

Bethel Business Solutions Transforming Dreams Into Reality

10 STEPS TO OWNING YOUR OWN TRUCKING FREIGHT BROKER/ AGENT BUSINESS

The primary goal is simply to have the

broker help lower the transportation costs of the shipper while allowing the shipper to focus on its internal operations.

Got freight ready to go? Here's how it moves-

1. A contract for carriage called a bill of lading is issued by the carrier. The bill of lading is attached to each freight load and follows each load through the supply chain.

The bill of lading describes the terms and condition of shipment. It tells who is responsible for the freight being shipped. While there may be other documents that accompany the negotiated process, the bill of lading represents the largest part of the carriage process.

The bill of lading may be the only carriage contract and may function as the delivery receipt or document of title.

2. In some cases the shipper contracts directly with a carrier or the shipper contracts with an intermediary, the broker. The broker is 'the middleman' who matches cargo from a shipper with a carrier in order to successfully accomplish the transportation requirement.

3. In some cases a shipper has not negotiated a contractual relationship with a carrier and cannot find an available carrier to haul its freight. The shipper may look to a broker for assistance.

Bethel Business Solutions Transforming Dreams Into Reality

10 STEPS TO OWNING YOUR OWN TRUCKING FREIGHT BROKER/ AGENT BUSINESS

4. The broker sends the freight bill to the shipper and pays the carrier.

5. Once the load is moved and the appropriate freight bills or invoices are sent and received, each party issues payment to the other to complete the transaction.

Where is the bottom line – the profit?

The difference between what is billed the shipper and what is paid the carrier serves as the broker's profit.

The broker must price its service high enough to cover the freight bill amount owed to the carrier but low enough to remain competitive.

If the broker's price charged is too low, the broker fails to make money on the transaction. If the broker's price charged is too high, the broker fails to retain the much needed business to other brokers.

Effective execution of the process details how the broker makes a profit. The broker must work to secure freight from the shippers that pay the broker more than what the broker will owe the carrier for executing carriage services.

If the shipper can obtain competitive rates from carriers and basically cover the load for the same rates offered through the broker, what

Bethel Business Solutions Transforming Dreams Into Reality

10 STEPS TO OWNING YOUR OWN TRUCKING FREIGHT BROKER/ AGENT BUSINESS

compels the shipper to seek the services of the broker?

You got it!!

Increase Your Business with Value-Added Service

The value-added service that a broker can provide that can encourage the supplier to use the services of the broker. Examples include -

1. Finding and dispatching carriers when the shipper does not have
time to arrange for the shipment. Because the shipper does not have to arrange for the transportation services on its own, the shipper may decide to do business with the broker.

2. Tracking and tracing the load from origin to destination and making the information readily available to the shipper.

3. Consolidating billing to the shipper that allows the shipper to receive summary bill that includes multiple shipments.

Carrier benefits too!

As a broker, a carrier may choose to work with your firm to acquire business he may not otherwise obtain. The availability of back haul load for carriers may seem appealing and profitable on a return trip.

Please be advised there are risk involved in

Bethel Business Solutions Transforming Dreams Into Reality

10 STEPS TO OWNING YOUR OWN TRUCKING FREIGHT BROKER/ AGENT BUSINESS

this business as there are risk involved in any business. To better understand your obligations and the obligation of all others - - you will need to attend the class.

Bethel Business Solutions Transforming Dreams Into Reality

10 STEPS TO OWNING YOUR OWN TRUCKING FREIGHT BROKER/ AGENT BUSINESS

STEP THREE
Abide by the Industry's Standards

As in every industry, there will be things that will happen, things that will go wrong and the hard decisions that must be made. Some will affect the bottom line of your business, your driver and maybe even the customer. Usually in the transportation industry as in others, issues will arise out of someone's improper decision-making and incorrect application of key ethics in business.

While ethics and morals both relate to right and wrong, **morals are established internally and ethics are external rules**. Ethics are a series of beliefs that society arrives at, chosen and adopted individually by each person. Morals are a societal idea that a specific action is evil or immoral and another specific action is good or moral.

Being ethical and trustworthy in the logistics industry as in any other business is imperative. You will be dealing with customers, carriers, and other business associates and your word is all you have. Confidence and trust must be present in order for your business and you to become successful.

If your company has spent thousands of dollars building a brand and a reputation in the industry and your promise to provide a service at a determined cost, and you cannot – you are etching your way into a position of not

Bethel Business Solutions Transforming Dreams Into Reality

10 STEPS TO OWNING YOUR OWN TRUCKING FREIGHT BROKER/ AGENT BUSINESS

being able to be trusted. Not only are

you committing to a disservice to your company you are destroying the reputation of your company. Clear up the problem as quickly as possible.

Here is a quick rule of success. Always be loyal to your company. When making decisions, you must always focus on one key issue – which decision is in the best interest of your company. Focus on what is advantageous financially, legally and operationally to your organization and what decision is best to achieve its goals.

In most businesses, we can agree that the primary focus is on making a profit. However, if done at the expense of other and other companies, you will likely find that if you conduct business with little or no regard for others, your industry-wide reputation in this service-providing industry will lead to a significant loss of business.

Means and ends refer to obtaining a result (end) and how you plan to achieve that outcome (means). While each of us acts a little differently in how we practice our personal "code of ethics," there are criteria for each organization in all industry that should remain intact by each of its agents. The criteria helps to secure that a good and credible job will be done by all.

A reminder – in your day-to-day business dealings you will come across people, companies,

Bethel Business Solutions Transforming Dreams Into Reality

10 STEPS TO OWNING YOUR OWN TRUCKING FREIGHT BROKER/ AGENT BUSINESS

drivers, repair centers, lumpers, carriers, and

customers willing to take part in unethical behaviors. Don't do it. Learn how to protect yourself from the lack of moral and unethical practices. Practicing business in an ethical manner will help you to enjoy a satisfying career in the transportation brokerage industry.

Even though the possibilities are unlimited, here are examples of some *unethical business practices* to look out for in your business efforts:

- **Unethical Carriers' Behavior** may try to falsify information such as insurance coverage limits, operating status, or other highly relevant information. They may "steal" or "back-solicit" the customer. Some carriers may hire drivers and not pay them. They may contract to pick up freight and leave you and your customer in a difficult problem if they choose to cancel without notification.

- **Unethical Customers' Behavior** may not pay the broker for services provided. They may arbitrarily deduct unforeseen revenue from the payment or book trucks not knowing for certain they will have freight to haul.

Bethel Business Solutions Transforming Dreams Into Reality

10 STEPS TO OWNING YOUR OWN TRUCKING FREIGHT BROKER/ AGENT BUSINESS

- **Unethical Brokers' Behavior** may book truck without knowing for certain that they will have freight to haul.

- They may misrepresent the carrier's reputation to the customer, insurance coverage, or the carrier's legal authority to carry freight. They may not pay invoices, pay invoices late, or attempt to underpay or deduct from legitimate charges. Brokers may contract to move freight then leave customers in a difficult position by cancelling without notification.

But, please don't be dismayed. We will cover methods, questions, and contracts to protect you from unethical practices. Remember morals and ethics are your reputation and that your reputation is vital in achieving business success.

If you work for a brokerage firm, you must keep its success in mind, and operate as such. That may mean passing on an opportunity that could be lucrative but presents ethical issues ahead. It should be the long-term interest of the company that becomes your top priority. Follow the rule of loyal and ethical behavior for your organization and you will help to ensure your career, your reputation, your company's brand and success as a whole.

You will be asked to make basic business decision every day in your dealing with the logistic trade. It is important to remember

Bethel Business Solutions Transforming Dreams Into Reality

10 STEPS TO OWNING YOUR OWN TRUCKING FREIGHT BROKER/ AGENT BUSINESS

that these decisions will have a long-term effect on your business, your company and you, whether positive or negative.

Terms to consider and remember when making decisions

Morals – society's view on right and wrong
Ethics – how a person chooses to use moral ideas
Autonomy – the ability to freely determine one's own course in life
Means and ends – the end result of decisions and the actions used to get there.

If the load is delivered without incidents, you should pay the carrier, even if the shipper does not pay you. This is the foundation of ethical business relationships and will likely serve to benefit you and your company in the long run.

Remember, it is doing what you say you will do regardless of its impact on immediate profitability is note of the true tests of ethics and morality.

Bethel Business Solutions Transforming Dreams Into Reality

10 STEPS TO OWNING YOUR OWN TRUCKING FREIGHT BROKER/ AGENT BUSINESS

STEP FOUR
Satisfy the Steps to Become an Agent

We are looking for highly motivated individuals to grow with us. This terrific opportunity is open for aggressive Freight Agents to join us. We are proud of the relationship we have with each of our partners throughout the United States.

You don't need your own current customer or carrier base. All you need to have is a desire to learn the fright broker business in real time. We are looking for motivated, independent, people with good work ethics and strong entrepreneurial spirit to work with us as an independent freight agent.

As an agent

You will receive an agreed upon minimum and maximum of the profit for all shipments with unlimited earnings potential.

Use of the company insurance and bonds

Use of the company brand name and online recognition

Direct deposit payment of your commissions

Technology you need for success

An opportunity to partner with a logistics company as an independent full-time Contractor (1099).

Bethel Business Solutions Transforming Dreams Into Reality

10 STEPS TO OWNING YOUR OWN TRUCKING FREIGHT BROKER/ AGENT BUSINESS

Do you have what it takes to run one of these businesses? Personality matters, but it is not something that cannot be learned. You may need some of the following traits:

Excellent Customer Services Qualities

Flexibility

Persistence and energy

Patience

Helpful experience

In additional to having personality, there is a range of skills and experience needed to run a business. When operating your business solo, you may need all of these characteristics to some degree.

As a general rule, you could benefit by having some kind of experience and understanding the concepts of **sales and marketing**. While you don't need a degree, it helps to be good at selling.

Determining your strengths

Take a list at the above list of character traits with yourself in mind. Which of these characteristics do you possess? Are you a take charge type person? Are you an organized whiz? How good are you at multitasking? What kind of experience do you have? What do you see as your major strengths and/or weaknesses?

Next think about the kind of lifestyle you

Bethel Business Solutions Transforming Dreams Into Reality

10 STEPS TO OWNING YOUR OWN TRUCKING FREIGHT BROKER/ AGENT BUSINESS

prefer. You must be able to wear many hats. A transportation brokerage industry agent or broker's life may constitute:

Long hours

Completing many task at one time

Communicating via telephone for many hours

Constant interruptions

Open lines of communications

Open-minded

Ability to follow through

With this position, you will be a 1099 independent freight agent and participate in efforts to grow and increase the market presence of your company as a premier freight transportation & logistic provider.

The main focus of the position is to build a solid client base of shippers and carriers. You will be in contact with client's daily, building relationships, solving problems, and assessing customer needs to make sure they are met along with the company's goals.

You will work with IT dispatch software and some other shipper database tools to help to locate and identify quality shippers and customers.

Bethel Business Solutions Transforming Dreams Into Reality

10 STEPS TO OWNING YOUR OWN TRUCKING FREIGHT BROKER/ AGENT BUSINESS

STEP FIVE
Understand the Industry's Work Environment

Gone are the days when freight brokers used ledger books to track their loads. Most pertinent information about a load was kept in a ledger book. All shipments were entered in the ledger and each shipment was given a progressive number. Each load included the ship date, delivery date, invoice date, invoice amount, agreed rate with the carrier, and amounts paid or to be paid to the carrier.

Today, in the transportation industry, many tools exist to assist a freight company, broker, agent, and drivers to keep track of the business. In the business of freight broker and agent for the transportation industry, equipment and technology go together hand in hand.

You may need:
- A computer in your office and being computer literate helps. Your computer should be equipped with -
- Internet service and you may find it necessary to produce memos, letters, financial invoices, reports and many others.
- A multiline-capable telephone is ideal. You may want to forward the line to another number such as an answering service or a cellular phone.
- Fax machine or a fax capability on a computer or a .pdf file in lieu of a fax.
- Additional software i.e. dispatch software can help if you plan to dispatch multiple

Bethel Business Solutions Transforming Dreams Into Reality

10 STEPS TO OWNING YOUR OWN TRUCKING FREIGHT BROKER/ AGENT BUSINESS
\

- loads per day.
- Carrier files retain a list of the qualifications applied to each carrier file. Files should always be complete. You may need to review it quickly every time a load is hauled.
- Shipper files should remain complete and updated with new contact information. Review frequently and modify information so that your office can better serve the client.

Other necessary office equipment may include a copier, file cabinets, a cellular phone, office space and location. Joining various industry groups and local traffic club can be informative and helpful. This will allow you to exchange information, contacts and ideas.

As you and your business continues to grow, you may want to include financial files composed of a general ledger, income statement or profit and lost statement, balance sheet, daily financial checklist, checkbook register, bank reconciliation, bill of lading, and 1099s.

For success in this business and in any business - time management is a must. Save time and use it to your benefit. The more time you save, the more you can accomplish. If it takes you three hours a week to balance your check book and write out your accounts payable checks, that may be several loads fewer than you have the opportunity to move freight. That could mean several hundred dollars less each month,

Bethel Business Solutions Transforming Dreams Into Reality

10 STEPS TO OWNING YOUR OWN TRUCKING FREIGHT BROKER/ AGENT BUSINESS

or several thousands of dollars per year.

You may choose to outsource some of the functions that are an integral part of your weakness or those that you find tedious.

Knowledge does not replace experience.

It is generally agreed that experience is based on practice and practice makes perfect. While practice may not always make perfect, it is necessary to make certain you recognize the value of experience in business. The people who specialize in specific types of services are experienced at their craft which is gained largely through practice. The term experience implies that a person has had many more experiences in a particular area than the typical person. You can always benefit from those who are more experienced and are willing to share their knowledge. This alone is reason enough to join various trade industry organizations and attend their meetings.

You can always learn something from someone who has had more or different experiences than you. If you choose not to listen and learn, then you may find yourself troubleshooting the same problem they have already solved. You can waste your time 'reinventing the wheel' or learn from your experienced partners' past experiences. Instead of reinventing the wheel, you should be making new and improved wheels that go twice as fast.

Bethel Business Solutions Transforming Dreams Into Reality

10 STEPS TO OWNING YOUR OWN TRUCKING FREIGHT BROKER/ AGENT BUSINESS

Experiences

The benefit of experience obtained by someone else can teach you many things that can save you liability headaches, regulatory

problems, and many other issues. Until you can run a brokerage with only a pencil and paper, until you can quote rates and lanes in 45seconds off the top of your head because you know where the trucks are, you have moved so much freight for so long that you are an expert, you should use every resource possible. Once you are that good and that familiar with the marketplace, you will be successful.

Your knowledge has become experience when you really understand freight flows and lanes. When you have you have the practical working knowledge of the supply and demand in most major metropolitan cities. When you can locate a city, town, or suburb on a map in a few seconds, when you have created accustom-tabbed or electronic Rolodex which contains contacts of every shipper, broker, and half the carriers throughout the United States you're experienced.

Acquiring knowledge is step one. You are attaining the knowledge. In order for the knowledge to help you become successful, you must use it. Learn everything you can about the industry you are operating n, and since it changes daily, realize this is not a one-time research project.

Bethel Business Solutions Transforming Dreams Into Reality

10 STEPS TO OWNING YOUR OWN TRUCKING FREIGHT BROKER/ AGENT BUSINESS

STEP SIX
Familiarize Yourself with Industry Terms

Every business has its own jargon or language and the logistic trade is no different. Here are common terms in the freight and transportation industry that you will want to become familiar with. You don't have to learn them all at once, just keep your booklet handy to serve as a guide.

As a broker, you must be aware of all modes of transporting freight. Included are terms for air, cargo railroad, and LTI freight. When negotiating for air, cargo railroad, and LTI freight these terms will serve useful.

Different brokers develop specific areas of expertise. A word to the wise - learn as much as you can about the area of brokerage for the company for which you work.

If a broker is dealing with a mode of transportation with which it is not familiar for example a trucking broker is asked by a shipper to expedite freight by way of air carriage, you have to refer the shipper to a freight broker who has experience for that particular mode of transportation.

It will be expected that you are able to communicate with a working knowledge and intelligently when contacted by a potential customer, even when referring the client to another freight broker.

Bethel Business Solutions Transforming Dreams Into Reality

10 STEPS TO OWNING YOUR OWN TRUCKING FREIGHT BROKER/ AGENT BUSINESS

International Commercial Terms (INCOTERMS) define the duties of the buyer and the seller at each step in the movement of international goods.

Here's a summary of INCOTERMS

Ex Works (EXW)- The seller makes the goods available at their docks. The buyer is responsible for all costs and risks involved in taking the goods from the seller's dock to the destination. This INCOTRTM provides minimum risk for the seller.

Free Carrier (FCA) - The seller fulfills their duties when the goods, cleared for export, are given to the carrier chosen by the buyer at a name place. The buyer assumes risk at the point of exchange and pays for all freight.

Free Alongside Ship (FAS) - The seller's obligation is to deliver the goods alongside the ship on the quay. The buyer then assumes all risks and costs from that point. The buyer must also provide export clearance.

Free on Board (FOB) - The seller delivers the goods to the ship and has fulfilled their duty when the goods pass over the ship's rail at the named port. This means that the seller pays for loading charges, pays for loading charges, pays freight charges to the named port and provides export clearance. The buyer bears all costs and risks from that point on.

Carriage Paid To (CPT) - The seller pays the

Bethel Business Solutions Transforming Dreams Into Reality

10 STEPS TO OWNING YOUR OWN TRUCKING FREIGHT BROKER/ AGENT BUSINESS

freight costs to the named destination as well as provides export clearance. Once the goods have been delivered to the carrier, risk is transferred to the buyer.

Carriage and Insurance Paid To (CIP) purchase cargo insurance in the name of the buyer while the goods are in transit to the named port of shipment. The seller must also pay loading costs, unloading costs if they are included in the freight, and provide export clearance.

Cost and Freight (CFR) – The seller arranges and pays for transportation to the named port of destination, but risk and any other costs while on the ship are passed to the buyer as the goods pass over the ship's rail at port of shipment. The seller must also pay loading costs, unloading costs if they are included in the freight, and provide export clearance.

Cost, Insurance, and Freight (CIF) – The seller not only has the identical obligations as in CFR but must provide marine insurance while the goods are in transit in the name of the buyer. The buyer may wish to purchase additional insurance the seller must provide only minimum coverage. At the port of destination, the buyer pays all unloading costs if they are already included in the freight and assumes all risks and costs from the port of destination.

Bethel Business Solutions Transforming Dreams Into Reality

10 STEPS TO OWNING YOUR OWN TRUCKING FREIGHT BROKER/ AGENT BUSINESS

Delivered at Frontier (DAF) – The seller fulfills his or her risk and costs duties when the goods are made available, cleared for export at the named point and placed at the

frontier, but prior to the customs border of the adjoining country. The buyer takes delivery at the named frontier.

Delivered Ex Ship(DES) – The seller meets his or her duties when the goods have been made available to the buyer on board the ship unclear for import at the named port of destination. All risk and costs involved in getting the goods to the named port of destination is the

seller's. The buyer takes delivery at the port of destination, pays unloading fees, and provides import clearance.

Delivered Ex Quay (DEQ) – This means that he seller meets his or her
obligations when the goods are made available to the buyer on the wharf (quay) at the named port of destination, cleared for importation. The seller assumes all risks and costs, including duties, taxes, and any other charges in delivering the goods. The buyer's obligation begins after taking delivery from the quay at port of destination.

Delivered Duty Unpaid (DDU) – The seller's duties end after the goods have been made available to the buyer at the named place in the country of importation. He or she has to pay the costs and assume the risks involved in bringing the goods to the named place of

Bethel Business Solutions Transforming Dreams Into Reality

10 STEPS TO OWNING YOUR OWN TRUCKING FREIGHT BROKER/ AGENT BUSINESS

destination. The buyer pays the duties, taxes, and fees. The buyer simply takes delivery of the goods at the named place and costs and risks transfer here. This is the maximum obligation that can be assumed by the seller.

Intermodal Freight or "multimodal" – means any shipment using two or multiple modes of freight transportation during the transport process.

Door to door – the broker will arrange for the transportation from the shippers dock to the receiver's door.

Less-than-Truckload – loads that require less space than the standard 53' or 48' trailer and weigh less than 10,000 pounds a full truckload at a least expensive mode of transportation.

Full Truckload – utilizing the standard trailer of 53' or 48' at a maximum weight of up to 80,000 pounds gross vehicle weight to operate in the United States.

Shipper – any source that hires a carrier to transport goods to a receiver.

Distribution Center (DC) – usually a large retail store will purchase freight from a manufacturer requesting the shipment be delivered directly. The DC may serve as a receiver or consignee for many truck load deliveries.

A third-party logistics (3PL) supply-chain participant provides a broad range of services to its client.

Bethel Business Solutions Transforming Dreams Into Reality

10 STEPS TO OWNING YOUR OWN TRUCKING FREIGHT BROKER/ AGENT BUSINESS

Just-In-Time (JIT) - some manufacturers ship raw materials and finished products that are time-sensitive with strict delivery guidelines that large fines are imposed upon for any delays.

While **JIT** freight does bring a bonus of a higher price, if ineffective performances of any type, these types of shipments can be disastrous if inadequate contracts or carriers.

Department of Transportation (DOT) - Department of Transportation

Types of Shippers

Refrigerated - "reefer" or refrigerated trailers - self-contained refrigerator and freezer units and used to haul perishable items that must be transported at a certain temperature. Some refrigerated trailers can be used to haul dry freight but others cannot because of trailer sizes and door-opening limitations. Refrigerated trailers are heavier than dry van trailers because of the added weight of the refrigeration units, so they cannot handle as much cargo as a dry van trailer. Used frequently in the transport of grocery and produce items.

Flatbed - a floor, with straps and braces to hold freight. Usually the flatbed offers little or no protection from the elements. Used primarily for trees, lumber, and large construction parts.

Bethel Business Solutions Transforming Dreams Into Reality

10 STEPS TO OWNING YOUR OWN TRUCKING FREIGHT BROKER/ AGENT BUSINESS

Owner-Operators In addition to trucking companies, there are independents owner-operators who own and operate a truck or several trucks and have carrier authority.

Types of Freight & Cargo

There are many types of shippers and carriers. Freight falls under some general categories but specific types of freight and the requirements for carrying the freight is endless.

Freight of all Kinds (FAK) - FAK is the largest category of freight which includes many different types of freight to include consumer goods and manufactured products. A good rule of thumb is if the product can be found in the Walmart store, it is probably FAK freight.

Foodstuff - While foodstuff can also be found in the Walmart stores, it is entered in a separate category all its own. Foodstuff is any perishable item that can be stored in a cabinet or panty space and is hauled in a dry van trailer. Quality and spoilage of foodstuffs can be burden to the trucking company.

High-Dollar Cargo - Cargo deemed at a greater risk for theft and damages. A term adopted by the cargo insurance industry and used by many carriers usually covers freight being hauled up to a value of $100,000. Carriers have increased the value of coverage to $250,000

Bethel Business Solutions Transforming Dreams Into Reality

10 STEPS TO OWNING YOUR OWN TRUCKING FREIGHT BROKER/ AGENT BUSINESS

or up to $500,000. Most of the high-dollar commodities are commonly excluded from cargo insurance policies. Additional cargo insurance premiums are typically charged to obtain the additional insurance.

Hazardous Materials – (Haz-Mat) According to the U. S. Department of Transportation (DOT)

defines hazardous waste material as a substance or material, including a hazardous substance, which has been determined by the Secretary of

Transportation to be capable of posing an unreasonable risk to health, safety and property when transported in commerce, and which has so been designated.

Haz-Mat includes any product that may be shipped that because of its contents or properties can cause loss of life or damage to property or the environment if involved in an accident.

Brokers involved with haz-mat transportation need to register with the DOT and meet training requirements. In order to haul hazardous materials, the carrier must be authorized by the FMCSA, under the DOT, and the driver must have a CDL license with a haz-mat endorsement.

Should a load of hazardous maters be involved in an accident, regardless of the seriousness of the accident or the class of the haz-mat product, and approved environmental clean-up group must be at the scene to assist in the de-containment and cleanup process. The cleanup process is expensive and payment for services

Bethel Business Solutions Transforming Dreams Into Reality

10 STEPS TO OWNING YOUR OWN TRUCKING FREIGHT BROKER/ AGENT BUSINESS

is the responsibility of whoever is at fault unless otherwise agreed upon in the carriage contract.

If the loss is due to an accident, the cost is usually the responsibility of the carrier. If the loss is due to improper packaging or loading, the cost could be the responsibility of the shipper.

There are other factors that may cause a trucking company to decide to find hazardous materials the too costly to handle. Other

reasons will be discussed in the class on logistic training.

Bill of Lading – a transportation document that is the contract of carriage between the shipper and carrier. It provides a receipt for the goods the shipper tenders to the carrier and may show certificate of title.

Broker – an intermediary between the shipper and the carrier. The broker arranges transportation for shippers and secures carriers to provide the actual truck transportation. A broker does not assume responsibility for the cargo and usually does not take possession of the cargo.

Common Carrier – A for-hire carrier that holds itself out to serve the general public at reasonable rates and without discrimination to operate, the carrier must secure a certificate of public convenience and necessity.

Bethel Business Solutions Transforming Dreams Into Reality

10 STEPS TO OWNING YOUR OWN TRUCKING FREIGHT BROKER/ AGENT BUSINESS

Connecting Carrier – a carrier that interchanges trailers with another transportation line

Dispatching – The carrier activities involved with controlling equipment, involves arranging for fuel, drivers, crews, equipment and terminal space.

Freight – any commodity being transported

Lumper – a person who assists a motor carrier driver in the loading and unloading of property and commonly used in the food industry.

<u>Hope you learned a lot. Remember you don't have to learn everything all at once. Keep your guidebook handy. Learn as you go.</u>

Bethel Business Solutions Transforming Dreams Into Reality

10 STEPS TO OWNING YOUR OWN TRUCKING FREIGHT BROKER/ AGENT BUSINESS

STEP SEVEN
Build the Steps to Become a Broker

This is a booming industry . . .

Although no number exist for this market, experts predict that the industry will continue to grow.

As a freight broker

We are prepared to offer talented, ambitious people with the opportunity to become top brokers in the business and to take your career to the next level.

As a freight broker you will earn substantial commissions and be in control as an independent contractor in control of your own business.

High energy and sales results that will inspire and motivate you to meet your goals as a freight broker and provide exceptional service to our clients.

If you are ready to make a positive and new transition of your broker agent career,

You must be -

Able to thrive in an environment where earnings potential is dictated by performance

Have a strong background in business-to-business outbound calling and sales

Bethel Business Solutions Transforming Dreams Into Reality

10 STEPS TO OWNING YOUR OWN TRUCKING FREIGHT BROKER/ AGENT BUSINESS

A positive, motivated can-do attitude

Must be aggressive, organized and effective under pressure

Competitive energy to excel beyond goal expectations and a desire to win

Strong negotiating and problem-solving skills

Excellent written and verbal communication skills

Ability to work independently

A proven sales background documented success and not afraid of monthly numbers

Demonstrated excellent time management, organizational and multitasking skills

Customer service approach with a sense of urgency

Unwavering integrity

Have a home computer, high speed internet, home phone & fax

You must be committed to:

Participate in efforts to grow the brokerage business and increase the market presence of your logistic company to be a premier freight broker and logistics provider

Bethel Business Solutions Transforming Dreams Into Reality

10 STEPS TO OWNING YOUR OWN TRUCKING FREIGHT BROKER/ AGENT BUSINESS

Build a solid client base of shippers and carriers. You will be in daily contact with building relationships, solving problems, and assessing the clients who need to meet along with company's goals

Ready to work immediately

Establish relationships with carriers and shippers

Solicit new shipper businesses

Solicit new carrier businesses

Conduct freight bidding and quoting

Manage customer relationships

Coordinates with administration to ensure that accounts are current

Prepare and coordinate required reporting documentation

Proactively manage exceptions and provide solutions between shippers and carriers

Communicate information timely and accurately

Broker

Another task you will need to accomplish is setting your office policies. The more thought you give to it early on, while your business is small, the better you will be able to handle growth later.

Bethel Business Solutions Transforming Dreams Into Reality

10 STEPS TO OWNING YOUR OWN TRUCKING FREIGHT BROKER/ AGENT BUSINESS

Make sure you decide on official policies for issues like business hours, customer service policies and procedures, housekeeping rules, security, incident reporting, documentation systems, management policies, new client welcome program and many more.

General Operations

Keeping your office running smoothly requires you to complete many different tasks simultaneously. Either in between customers or after hours, you'll be organizing your notes, files and other pertinent information, cleaning, straightening and replenishing paper supply items, ordering supplies, documenting receipts, bookkeeping, documenting time spent, checking on the drivers, answering the telephone, and a whole host of other tasks, many of which are noticeable only if they do not get done.

Maximizing Cash Flow

There are several ways to make sure you have enough money available for running your business. Most of them involve vigilance. Try these strategies:

Watch your expenditures

Look for ways to save money

Keep an eye on your accounts receivable

Keep your overhead low

Borrow ahead

Bethel Business Solutions Transforming Dreams Into Reality

10 STEPS TO OWNING YOUR OWN TRUCKING FREIGHT BROKER/ AGENT BUSINESS

Put the money back into the business

Be cautious

Document, document, document

Use a planner

Keep well-ordered files

Organize your information

Write out detailed policies & procedures

Bethel Business Solutions Transforming Dreams Into Reality

10 STEPS TO OWNING YOUR OWN TRUCKING FREIGHT BROKER/ AGENT BUSINESS

STEP EIGHT
Consider the Big Picture

Other growing trends you may want to consider in the transportation freight and logistic business could include . . .

Excellent Customer Service

Even though you may not deal with customers face-to-face, you still need to give them good customer service. Here are a few aspects specific to business:

> Provide quick and timely service –
> Respond promptly to queries
> Acknowledge orders
> Check for incomplete transactions
> Notify customers of timelines
> Stay connected with your clients – shippers and carriers
> Cheerful attitude
> Personal approach
> Dedication
> Innovation

The most successful way to build a business is by recommendations. Studies show that although advertising in the Yellow Pages, on the internet, and through the mail can result in a lot of inquires those do not reliably translate to sales. However, recommendations are much more effective.

Bethel Business Solutions Transforming Dreams Into Reality

10 STEPS TO OWNING YOUR OWN TRUCKING FREIGHT BROKER/ AGENT BUSINESS

Many entrepreneurs will tell you 'word of mouth' is the most important way to become known. Enlist the help of your friends and relatives to get the word out. Words quickly spread. Don't be afraid to ask them to help spread the word about your new business.

Often it doesn't take much. Word of mouth is the best kind of advertising. So make it work for you. Here are a few ideas you may want to use:

Customer testimonials: When you get a super satisfied customer or client who compliments the way you handle his business, ask if you can quote that person in your company's website or information. Most people will be happy to allow this.

Driver's praises: Maybe one of your drivers or associates is fascinated by the way you troubleshoots an unforeseen problem quickly and diligently. Ask if the praise can be included in your information. You will be surprised at the type of interest and business such praises can attract for your office.

Vendor or manufacturer endorsements: These can be put into your information as well especially if a vendor or manufacture company is well-known.

Bethel Business Solutions Transforming Dreams Into Reality

10 STEPS TO OWNING YOUR OWN TRUCKING FREIGHT BROKER/ AGENT BUSINESS

Make Your Business Shine

Provide excellent customer service

Exceed expectations

Guard your reputation

Be reliable and resourceful

Keep learning

Stay well - informed

Join professional organizations

Learn from others

Look toward the future

Evaluate your progress

Have I carefully analyzed demand and adjusted to change?

Have I kept good control of overhead cost and maximized my resources?

Are my cash reserves sufficient?

Does my company or office provide the kind of customer service that keeps clients coming back?

Above all, remember why you got into the industry or into any business in the first place and what you want to accomplish in it!!!

Bethel Business Solutions Transforming Dreams Into Reality

10 STEPS TO OWNING YOUR OWN TRUCKING FREIGHT BROKER/ AGENT BUSINESS

Be a good citizen, employee, and client.

Deliver what you promise.

Deal fairly with others.

Enjoy what you do.

Learn the skills you need to be a successful and profitable Freight Broker:

Recognize the progression of freight brokering from start to finish

Have the tools needed to be successful and effective as a freight agent

Learn the essentials of day-to-day operations and tasks of a freight brokering as an agent

Use techniques and skills such as prospecting, sales, marketing, freight costs and negotiations

Be able to accomplish and manage a freight shipment from origin to destination

Gain valuable and knowledgeable freight industry resources and assets with us

This is an ideal home-based career opportunity

Bethel Business Solutions Transforming Dreams Into Reality

10 STEPS TO OWNING YOUR OWN TRUCKING FREIGHT BROKER/ AGENT BUSINESS

This booklet serves as an overview and does not in any way represent the abridge publication containing all of the necessary information necessary for a successful career in the logistic business. It does however get you started.

AVAILABLE FOR A LIMITED TIME ONLY!!!

Bethel Business Solutions Transforming Dreams Into Reality

10 STEPS TO OWNING YOUR OWN TRUCKING FREIGHT BROKER/ AGENT BUSINESS

STEP NINE
Discover Self Pace & Time Management Success

We've all heard the saying "time is money", and that phrase is essentially true. Unfortunately, time doesn't always equal money though. Time is continually passing but that doesn't mean you are continually making money, this depends on how you manage your time and what you do with it. Here are 9 reasons time management is important.

9 Reasons Why Time Management is Important

1. **Time is limited**

   Everyone gets the same amount of time each day, and it's limited, therefore it's important to make the most of your time if you ever want to be more than average at the workplace.

2. **Accomplish more with less effort**

   By taking control of your time, you're able to stay focused on the task at hand. This leads to higher efficiency since you never lose momentum. Imagine running a mile where you stop every 5 seconds, this would cause you to become exhausted very quickly and take much longer to complete the run.

Bethel Business Solutions Transforming Dreams Into Reality

10 STEPS TO OWNING YOUR OWN TRUCKING FREIGHT BROKER/ AGENT BUSINESS

3. **Make better decisions**

   There are many choices in life and often-times we're faced with many choices to choose from at

   the same time. When you practice good time management, you have more time to breathe; this allows you to determine which choices are the best to make.
   When you feel pressed for time and have to make a decision, you're more likely to jump to conclusions and not fully consider the different options; this leads to poor decision making.

4. **Be more successful**

   Time management is the key to success; it allows you to take control of your life rather than follow the flow of others. You accomplish more, you make better decisions, and you work more efficiently; this leads to a more successful life.

5. **Learn more**

   When you control your time and work more efficiently, you're able to learn more and increase your experience faster. There's a reason some

   students graduate earlier than others, so imagine implementing time management throughout your entire career. You'll not only stand out from the rest, but you'll gain experience must faster and be able to move up in life a lot sooner.

6. **Reduce stress**

   One of the main causes of stress is due to people feeling rushed. The phrase "I have so much to do and so little time to do it" is

Bethel Business Solutions Transforming Dreams Into Reality

10 STEPS TO OWNING YOUR OWN TRUCKING FREIGHT BROKER/ AGENT BUSINESS

generally spoken with frustration which leads to stress. With good time management, you know how much time you have, how long it will take to get your tasks done, you accomplish more, and have more free time. This gives you more

breathing room, which reduces the feeling of being rushed, which in turn leads to less frustration and stress.

7. **Higher quality work**

We all need some free time to relax and unwind but, unfortunately, many of us don't get much free time because we're too busy trying to keep up with our daily activities and work load. By implementing time management skills, you are able to get more done in a shorter period of time leading to more free time.

8. **Creates discipline**

When you practice good time management in your life, you are less likely to procrastinate. Time management leads to higher productivity and leads to a disciplined life.

9. - See more at: http://www.appointment-plus.com/articles/why_time_management_is_important.php#sthash.lsqlrDjU.dpuf

Bethel Business Solutions Transforming Dreams Into Reality

10 STEPS TO OWNING YOUR OWN TRUCKING FREIGHT BROKER/ AGENT BUSINESS

STEP TEN
Bethel Business Solutions- Start Up

You are now ready to start your own freight broker business. If you need assistance with forming your business structure LLC, INC, Logo, Website, Business Plan etc. BBS can help!

Bethel Business Solutions is committed to develop the best freight broker in the business. We are devoted to provide a working atmosphere which allows each and every member of staff to have a job satisfaction at the same time produce the best quality freight broker services available for our customers.

Bethel Business Solutions leading in Business solutions!

Our mission is to provide our clients with the opportunity and tools to successfully start their dream job, business, or career. We pride ourselves on transforming dreams into reality.

We pride ourselves on transforming dreams into reality. Our mission is to provide our clients with the opportunity and tools to successfully achieve their dream career or launch their business passion.

Bethel Business Solutions Transforming Dreams Into Reality

10 STEPS TO OWNING YOUR OWN TRUCKING FREIGHT BROKER/ AGENT BUSINESS

The vision of Bethel Business Solutions is to assist every client from vision to reality. We assist and serve at each step providing significant services from start-up to completion. Our expert advice include business and personal must haves such as credit restoration, branding, website design, documentation acquisition, business certifications, business start-up capital, and logo design. It is our goal for all clients to leave empowered and enriched.

If you would like to start your own Freight Broker business and need assisting contact BBS and if we can assist you , We have affiliates that can assist with all phases from Insurance, DOT, FMCSA, etc.

Bethel Business Solutions Transforming Dreams Into Reality

10 STEPS TO OWNING YOUR OWN TRUCKING FREIGHT BROKER/ AGENT BUSINESS

About the Author

Alicia Griffin is an entrepreneur with over 13 years of start-up business experience whether profit or charitable businesses. She has owned many successful businesses across the United States to include Florida and Alabama. She specializes in various industries to include financial services, retail, grass root marketing, journalism, publication, interior design, and janitorial services.

Alicia attributes the vast background in entrepreneurship to the achievement of her success. Her experiences have allowed her a panoramic viewing, thus designing a plan to assist other business owners with achieving their greatest success.

In May of 2010 Alicia was diagnosed with stage 3B Colorectal Cancer. Her battle and defeat of cancer inspired her to partner with Lavette Johnson start a foundation Pretty Laces Pretty Faces Foundation. Pretty Laces Pretty Faces would serve to women from all walks of life who have lost their hair through diseases such as Cancer, Alopecia and other diseases to feel beautiful by offering wigs and hair pieces.

Bethel Business Solutions grew from Alicia's desire to help others aspiring to be successful business owners. Over the past 15 years, she has acquired proven knowledge that she believes she should share with her global neighboring business family.

Bethel Business Solutions Transforming Dreams Into Reality

10 STEPS TO OWNING YOUR OWN TRUCKING FREIGHT BROKER/ AGENT BUSINESS

In 2013 Alicia Griffin released her second book, *Diagnosis: Cancer | Rx: How My Journey of Faith Made Me Whole*. The book is available in Barnes and Nobles and local bookstores.

She is the wife of a freight carrier, mother, author, and successful business woman. She spends countless hours volunteering, is involved in business and trade associations. Her passion is for young women who may view hopelessness as an option. She has started a charitable organization *Hidden Treasures* to help girls ages 11-24 years old to improve their quality of life.

Carol Williams Ransom is a writer, producer, executive editor for a local publication. She holds a Bachelor Degree in Mass Communication from University of South Florida, a Master Degree in Organizational Management and Leadership from Springfield College and is presently a candidate for the terminal degree of PhD in Psychology from Northcentral University.

She is passionate about community and dedicates time as a community activist seeking justice. An advent gardener, Carol loves spending time with her grandchildren and God dog Nila.

She enjoys all phases of writing and editing to include plays, drama, soap opera or serial drama. She is a servant and dedicates time as a ghostwriter to assist others to write and share their story.

Bethel Business Solutions Transforming Dreams Into Reality

10 STEPS TO OWNING YOUR OWN TRUCKING FREIGHT BROKER/ AGENT BUSINESS

```
Other  Books  Authored  By:  Alicia
Griffin
```

Bethel Business Solutions Transforming Dreams Into Reality

www.ingramcontent.com/pod-product-compliance
Lightning Source LLC
LaVergne TN
LVHW022142230425
809465LV00026B/560